a dim sum of the day before

a dim sum of the day before
Steven Schroeder

Library of Congress Control Number: 2009939401
ISBN: 978-0-9824405-6-8
© Steven Schroeder, 2010

Ink Brush Press
inkbrushpress.com
Manufactured in the United States of America
Temple, Texas

Acknowledgments

Some of these poems first appeared in *TriQuarterly, Cha: An Asian Literary Journal, Macao Closer, Left Facing Bird, New Poetry Appreciation* (in Chinese translations by Li Sen and Wang Hao), *The Christian Science Monitor,* and steven-schroeder.blogspot.com.

Contents

written in passing

Mao's ghost wondering...1
concrete cold..4
avian flu advisory..5
no words...6
written in passing, written in stone............................7
floating lives.. 11
counting... 12
not about politics.. 13
torch bearers... 15
without silence.. 16
after an apocalypse...17
sing..18
empty talk.. 19
waiting to be born.. 21

still falling

three short exercises in Mohist logic.........................25
so many ways to fly..28
emphysema, slowly..29
another dance..30
still falling..31
you can smell roads..34
Lolita (a meditation on the hero) 35
to wait...36
a moment... 37
motions of memory..38
qi..41
above it all...42

the calisthenics of rain

a sign of the times, two times......................................45
guidebook says.. 47
a water planet...48
a sign..49
a peculiar song...50
southern cold..51
Gateway, Hong Kong...52
the calisthenics of rain..53
no denying it.. 58
even when...60
it goes without saying...61
all parallels and perpendiculars..................................62
year of the rat... 64

water music

for the light.. 71
a kind of meditation..76
one noble truth...77
bouganvillea..78
no fear..79
water music... 80
twelve songs, two mornings...82
In a Village Near Kunming...84
conversation..86
our own exile...87
a matter of sound...88
Morning..89
signs... 90

written in passing

Mao's ghost wondering
猫毛

1

Gray tabby slips under a chair
at the empty table next to mine
silent, waits.

I use the only Chinese
words I know I think might
interest a cat. She smiles

at *miao*, blinks at the mention
of her name. But *kitty kitty* is fine
too. And she doesn't mind small

talk in English. She is polite
about the cheese I offer,
but does not touch the corn.

She would prefer meat, but she
is here now for a presence, and I will

do. When I leave, her eyes close
in the momentary absence of a kiss.

2

Young cat, orange and white, follows the wall
this morning, but fast. He is not secure
in his invisibility, and it is true
that the flurry of orange fur
against white wall weathered gray
could turn heads. But no one else has taken
notice, and there is less danger in being seen
than a young cat might admit first thing in the morning.

At the other end of the walk, gray tabby has no doubt
she is out of sight slow against a low
wall. The third eye of her ear barely turns
when my step changes for a moment
at the sight of her. But she is sure
the gray cat I think I saw is
a figment of my imagination.

Her ear is a periscope that turns on
the world humans occupy, but she moves
in a space that is not there,
where there is no danger.

3

most cats here have nothing to say
most say it wisely walking away
when they meet strangers on the street
they are making space between them for a city

4

Since pinyin so often arrives toneless
and I so often compound toneless with tone
deaf, the ear's universe of meaning is
almost as wide as meaningless
but for the rhythm of it.

Speakers of *putonghua* never mistake
the late Chairman for a cat, but I do
so often with joy, delighted
that every cat I meet on the street
could be his ghost wondering
how on earth it came to this.

concrete cold

Trees planted when these stones were set in place
have grown old beneath them. Stones have scars
to show for it, broken lines that trace
the progress of roots across a mortar
grid too regular for life to bear.
Two days ago, before a flood,
crews took up dozens of them where
roots had wandered to the surface, made
soil explicit with roots in it and piles of them
to step over. Today, roots have been hacked away.
Stones will be reset, broken when
life goes on. And its melody
will always lie in what will never stand
for the concrete cold of a simple grid.

avian flu advisory

Watching sparrows
snatch flying things
I cannot see
from air so thick
they swim in it,
it is hard to think of them
as death threats. This patio
is insect-free. The birds
beating wings fast as they can
to be still for the moment
necessary to pluck an
insect from flight
are virtuosos
of fly fishing,
a morning floor show
worth the risk.

They tap dance
on the translucent roof
while mayflies chant
*there can be no pleasure
where there is no danger.*

no words

Pink and purple petunias mass with masses
on the boulevard waiting for buses
that pause in fleets where signs promise
they will stop. People in suits burst from nowhere,
sprint to catch one bus or the other leaving.
Patient petunias are never late. We are
waiting like people gracefully posturing
in the park, not waiting for the bus.
On a side street of abandoned shops
a crowd of people and dogs has gathered
on edges to watch an old hound circle
in the street, dying, silent. He may have been
hit, though there is no blood. He may have chosen
this place to die. He may be dying here by chance.
But I have no words to ask what happened. The dogs,
who have no more words than I, tell me more than
the people who do. There is nothing to be done.
The old hound circles, circles soundless –
no words for what happens. Some of us,
staggered by how easy it is to walk away from dying
when there is nothing to be done, will. But the crowd
will watch until the old hound dies, waiting.

written in passing, written in stone

1

Rain leaves
a record
of its falling
when a storm
passes. Lines

of green that
interrupt
the grid
of the walk
turn yellow dry

slow to brown.
Lines of leaves
follow wind
that brought them
down on rain.

Green to dry to slow
to brown, their spectrum
is history written

in passing,
written
in stone.

2

A break in the rain.
A man in a suit
stands on the edge

of a garden
on a hard path where
there is no danger

of mud on his shoes
with two gardeners
who know every plant

by name. He
stretches his hand
over the scene,

rebukes the storm.
Gardeners wait,
eyes on broken limbs

and fallen blossoms, hope
this break is long enough
to outlast the boss,

to give them time
to get their hands in the mud
to see what can be done.

3

Umber clouds roll
over sky that has
turned night

blue since
I last looked up
from a page waiting

to be turned.

4

Leaves finally despair of inscribing rain
on the surface of this walk. They fell in
waves when rain fell, lined up with prevailing
wind so you could read it in their lie as
you stepped over them. But another wave
fell and the simple lie of leaves became
a palimpsest with layers to decode.

Readers of leaves
who step over these
see a confusion of rain
falling in a riot of color.

Sweepers, who have no patience
for history, hurry them
into clusters to be
carted away
before they dry.

Readers see riots
of color confusions
of rain falling refugees

swept aside to make way
for the business of the present.

floating lives

All that climbing to forget a mountain
is no more than an emblem
at the intersection of ten thousand
floating lives.
            We tell ourselves the place
we stand is solid ground while we count corpses
that say it never was. It never
has been. Under the weight of all
these broken lives whisper *war*
is the luxury we cannot afford. Our lives
depend on fragile performances of humanity
fleeting as the floating mountains
on which, always disappointed,
we always stake them.

counting

Rain arrives as ordered on the first day
of mourning, gray sufficient
for thirty thousand, silent, and counting.

Counting. They say birds vanished,
left the sky without song
before the earth broke
on the crest of a slow wave
rolling plains to mountains. The whole
world shuddered at the immensity of silence.

Far from the center, birdsong and voices
on cellphones contain what is left
of silence, weave it into webs

to calm the earth shell of a rolling ocean
we mistook for solid ground.

Shenzhen, 19 May 2008

not about politics

but every person
who stops on the street
for a photo to prove
he was here stands
under a flag

one in three
has a red rectangle
with five yellow
stars on a cheek

and the boulevard
is lined with them

a cluster gathers
around a speaker
and a drum
raising fists
chanting in time
with the beat

and three flags wave
in front of them

a man makes a video
of the torch on a television
monitor by the walk

pointing his camera
at the screen
filming film
so he will have
the story of a story
not politics
to take home
a story of a story
about being somewhere
draped in one flag
or another

waiting for the torch
Shenzhen, 8 May 2008

torch bearers

Sticky flags make faces in the crowd
an ocean of red laced with yellow
stars, every head that bows or nods a flag

waving. Every parade makes its own
army, and flags underfoot the day after
this one are reminders that an army
rarely knows what it is walking on.

A week after they have fallen, they are
gone. Their not being there is a sign.

Flags take place as though they have always
been in it, but in the end women on their knees
scrape remnants off paving stones
so no one will walk on the flag without thinking.

without silence

Half a step out of step, butterfly
braces against prevailing wind.
A lifetime in the place, and still she
does not know the language. She can't

put silence between words out of mind,
stumbles on it every time she flies, feels
like she is falling. Sparrows tell her time
and time again she would be fluent

if she would learn to fall without
silence. They have no ear for nothing,
but she is sure the music would die
without it. She is fluent in

what is not said. Every flight
is a staggering conversation in it.

after an apocalypse
China 2008

All public celebration is
canceled for three days
of mourning, but the trees

on *nan hai da dao*
can't resist a confetti shower
after rain. They scatter

yellow rainbows where
we walk, remember
the dead but dance for

the living, shower
each going on
with flowers.

They have lived after
seasons of dying before.
They know ends

are fashioned from fragments
gathered in the shattered
middle of things that will not last.

sing

No call to deny some Messiah
three times when the world is nothing
but denial. There is no denying
what must be done, Gautama, when
suffering bursts into flame at Jokhang's gate,
circles silent with a dog dying
on a forgotten street in Shekou. No
denying the world denying power
to turn. No denying the world denying
power to act. No denying the world
denying power to speak. No denying
the world. In the beginning, no word. No
denying the first stone cast by someone
who is not without sin. No denying Spinoza.

The stone falling would think itself free
if it could think. If it could sing, it would
sing a song of freedom, fall harmless
at the feet of an army no less
an army when a soldier, bloodied
by a stone, steps from the ranks. The stone
falls, singing. There is no denying the song.

empty talk

*"The rioters who wore cassocks were no real monks
and what they did is completely against Buddhist codes,"
said Ngawang Daindzin, a living Buddha.
       All in all, it's China's Tibet, now and forever.
            Xinhua, 19 March 2008*

*Empty talk endangers the nation.
Practical work brings prosperity.
            a billboard in Shekou*

There are living Buddhas
on every side of every war. Nothing
they do changes the coming into being

of it, the passing away of it.
Passing away catches the eye: bodies
count, the slow awakening

of corpses piled high
while cities burn.
Ten thousand Buddhas see

what is not there
after the city has died. But not
anger burning slow under

occupation, not
impatience at the slow
curve of a twisted universe turned,

one in ten thousand Buddhas
chants, to justice.
Resigned to the slow turn

of a world still
turning, all the time
in the world is occupied

with no. States
line up living Buddhas
like barricades, tip them

like buses in burning streets, check
body counts, silence what is
out of line, contain

slow burns off stage so
nobody shouts fire until
all that is left is ashes.

...on the fifth anniversary of the U.S. occupation of Iraq

waiting to be born

A woman who has had enough
lies on the walk between two
climate controlled malls as though
it were a womb and she waiting to be

born. Sun has been
up no more than
an hour, but heat is
so heavy every step has to be

willed against the whole weight of it. She
has been carrying the dirty blanket she
lies on for days wrapped around what little she
has, now piled behind her head. Walkers step around her

hurrying somewhere without taking
notice, getting to work on time, meeting
deadlines, keeping

things moving, waiting
to be born again.

still falling

three short exercises in Mohist logic

白馬非馬

1

this
is
this

that
is
that

there

you
have
it

this
this

is
not
that

that
that

is
not
this

but

how
to
say

this
that

that
this

without

here
this
there
that

now
then
pointing?

2

Nothing common
about ground
below nobody's
sky, but there is
something to be said
for keeping the rain
on the other side,
keeping this side
dry. This

is this
that is

that and it goes
without saying
a white horse is

a white horse
not a horse

of a different color.

3

no this is
rain that is
not earth air fire all
water

so many ways to fly
for Liang Huichun

that bird did not choose you when
she nested in flowers at your window
but when she flew

ninety thousand miles is
nothing to your heart
wind below

blue sky
dry
cicada

laughter rises
on morning heat
far away

dove chuckles
so many
ways to fly

a nest is no more
than the passing
body of an absence

empty, she
soars

emphysema, slowly

Morning. You can look the sun in the eye
with no fear of blindness. Every driver
here on the way to some there has come out
of a cave this morning, knows more *daos* that
go nowhere than you can count, needs no time
to see shadows. It's shadows all the way.
This light does not change a thing, rises with
ten thousand buses, ten thousand trucks. Cars
couple at night, double while the city
multiplies, penetrates breath by breath, two,
four, eight, and soon there is more than ten
thousand times ten thousand lungs can breathe.
Every river of it flows into some sea,
and seas flow over us, breathless.

another dance

Black dog likes the sound
of my feet on paving stone,
picks up the pace, falls

into it, slips on
a new step, dances
a universe he might

inhabit, tries it on
for size, turns at a voice
from one he does, pauses

till it catches him,
knows his goddess
by her step,

settles home
until another
dance draws him in.

still falling

1

Not even mist, really. Water
so much a part of air
it is no surprise to swim

in it, forget to open
the umbrella you carry until
it has soaked you through. Sound

reminds you time broken is still
falling, fragments drumming
on a window somewhere

or a roof you think will keep you
dry while birds who have forgotten
too sing as though sun will

shine in no time. Look up
from morning coffee and the world
is covered in it. Now it is rain.

2

Three days of rain without a break has flooded the streets
with odors almost familiar – like what we know
but tilted on an axis of putrefaction.
Rats come up for air, wallow in it, while walkers

who can barely hold their heads above the flood
ford it like refugees crossing a river to another life.

3

Sparrows have had enough
of rain. They've invaded this
gazebo to preen on rafters
under a roof almost dry.

Damp rises even where rain
fall is broken. Ruffled
feathers contain it like
the pages of a book

that curl around the music
of their words and will not lie
flat where everything they'd hoped
to hide has been washed out of them.

4

Rain's fallen steady for a week, but sweepers
are on the street when they think sun should be
rising. Straw brooms hurry red earth in water
to edges of grass already sated with it. Tree
has fallen where mud can no longer
bear it, rising roots upturned beside the
path. Walkers weave around the tangle
of its branches. Umbrellas wilt under

rain and rising rain repeated until
at last they are neither here nor there.

Masses embrace the flood, let umbrellas fall,
resign themselves to water rising. Water,
the one mass rising here – the only revolution
red earth turning in a slow drain after days of rain.

you can smell roads

Walls flow like rivers here
slow to sea that backs away
from a city growing
unfamiliar fast,

waves of them marked
by towers that have less
to guard than when they
saw that nobody crossed

nothing on the city's edge, lost
in landfill and bridges. In the gardens
of the rich you can smell roads
where rivers ran. Now

oyster fishermen's huts have given way
to tents, and you know they will not be here long.

The ocean would not know the place
if it swept past walls to where it was
before. Rich people haunt the sea. A wall
rises with their dwelling on each new
coast, leaves traces of what was out of place
lost under layers of a young city growing old.

Lolita (a meditation on the hero)

树梨花压海棠

No surprises
here, nothing
but miracles.

A bagpiper
on the square
in woolen
socks and kilt
only a hero
could wear
in afternoon heat.

Everywhere
the sound
of people
walking
on water

and I think
an overbearing pear
might just meet its match
in the delicate blossoms
of a crabapple.

to wait

Old woman with a begging bowl rises
when the crowd rises
to wait for a bus

that will take them places
to move money. Her smile says
she knows excess

will spill over
on her
if she waits.

she lifts
her bowl.
I pass

she drops
a poem
in mine

we wait

a moment

Street corner alchemists are at war
with buses. Diesel makes things move;
but they mix it with simples to distill
metal so pure it will stop things
at the scene they have made
of wheels and carts and fire, home
passersby can smell where air is heavy
with elsewhere. Bicycle barricades
direct traffic under the noses of cops
who think they are in control.

Hover over it and it is an eddy
in the steady stream of this
diesel fired city. On the ground, it is
a moment that will not stand for no.

motions of memory

The time will come when our silence will be
more powerful than the voices you strangle today.
           August Spies

1

At Shekou Walmart, street lamps
wave red flags, and nobody gathers
to sing the *Internationale*.

They've rounded up the rats
on *Nanhai da dao*
for the holiday,

and Garden City Mall
has cautiously conspired
to mass pink flowers

in the ocean of red
that lines the escalator
outside Starbucks.

Dao ke da feichang dao
Dao ke dao feichang dao

Voices still,
silence, small, will
carry on, nameless.

2

We go through motions of memory
here, but May Day conversation
at McDonald's is more likely
to turn to American Idol than
Haymarket if it turns to America
at all. Someone may
have something to say
about thugs at CNN, but
today's *Internationale* is a medley
of pop songs to shop by. Albert and Lucy
are no more on the minds of common folk
here than in Forest Park. No idea
of an uprising. No idea
there were cadres in Chicago
when Saint Petersburg was still
waiting for dreamers to dream them.

Three days off for the middle class
to shop while workers who keep things moving
keep moving, still
waiting.

Forgetting is a motion of memory.

3

Welders working late on May Day
make a light show for crowds passing
eight stories below. Streets empty
in morning are full of night
people who take sparks in stride
without a second thought for dry
leaves where weather always falls
and nothing is likely to burn.

Heat and humidity slow every
sweltering thing to a pace so cold

no one cares when
the pianist in the bar
misses a note now and then.

They catch her drift, and
the idea of a melody
is enough for now.

qi

Six billion inner peaces perfectly
synchronized might prove simpler than a truce
negotiated on some battlefield.

Clusters in every clearing here go through
motions while the city is still drowsy
with morning. A woman kneels for a talk

with a white dog that has been a few steps
ahead of her and must have committed
some infraction that escaped me. He takes

the lecture with a smile and a drooping
tongue, eyes on the walk where there are people
to watch. Every morning, there is a wall

of carcasses to step over where a truck
backs to the edge of the sidewalk
to unload. Over these dead bodies

in and out among the living, every walker
dances on the delicate edge of *qi*
that gathers from all sides. Like the woman

dancing with an imagined sword under
a sign that says *Hangzhou Cuisine*, like the birds
dancing songs over the noise of the city rising,

like a single moment dancing in the clearing
of a truce negotiated on some battlefield.

above it all

Look east and you'd swear you could see mountains
on the far side of the bay. Climb them
dreaming *Qomolangma*, though,
and you'll still be so close to ocean
the gravity of it will make you think
flying out of the question. Ocean
will not let you forget you live
on a liquid planet. Even mountains
hover like spirits on the surface
of water. Coral at two thousand meters
is a sign the sky's a trick here.
You imagine yourself above it all,
but every clearing is ocean floor under
a wait of ten thousand fathoms or more.

the calisthenics of rain

a sign of the times, two times

Time is money, efficiency is life.
   sign at the corner of Gong Ye First Road and
   Nanhai da dao, Shekou, May 2008

1

The ghost of some hermit
among trees on the hillside
over Shekou Bar Street
watching workers
do the whole
thing over again
might have been
a prostitute, might have been
a monk, might have been
my imagination.

Time is
time, spent
or not.

Efficiency is another matter.

2

Only a foolish generation
asks for a sign when the air's thick with them,
no one asking. A sign of the times

is a sign of money. Taylor won
every revolution of the last
century. Lenin and Deng were

vanguards of a revolution
that made the world safe for
technocracy, dangerous for

anything but. Repeat
time is time time and time
again. Throw yourself

like a little tramp
into the works. Wander
when you have time (not

money). But the fact remains:
Where Have all the Flowers Gone? is
muzak with Pete Seeger's voice

missing, between *Feelings*
and *Love Story.* The engineers
have inherited the earth.

guidebook says

Typhoon mumbles something
about coming to Guangdong
in a language of waves
and steady rain that grows
stronger as the day passes. It hangs
offshore, feet shuffling like a tourist
running out of time
torn between sights
the guidebook says must not be
missed, keeps talking
rain that has everyone carrying
umbrellas and anticipation, thinking
about what has to be tied down
before the wind rises.

a water planet

On clear days, Hong Kong is a white line
of mushrooms rising straight-stemmed brown-rimmed
on a scrap of blue that skirts the long bridge.

Yesterday, it was a bank of dark clouds
glowing red with three days of rain
towering over cities on both sides

to remind every living thing in them
how small we are, how little we know
of a water planet we inhabit

like insects on a dry leaf
floating on the surface of a pond.

a sign

No naked light on an oil tanker in
Hong Kong Harbour is
a preemptive confession.

When it burns (as it knows
it will), light will be clothed
in the aftermath of it. Sun

will become an object of desire,
imagined brilliant on every
morning horizon, possibility

not illumination
in the spirit it scatters formless
on the surface of these waters.

a peculiar song

They have drained the pond
where the flamingos stay. Still

birds turn the heads of passersby
with their singing. A woman

stops to find one, and a dozen
others follow her eyes

up to a peculiar song. One
bird sings the absence
of a pink crowd
always present.

southern cold

Just a glimpse of mountains
from the train and the city
in lights already. I have come
to think of it as a moment
on the way to China, not
the thing itself; and I wonder
at southern cold, machine cold
too efficient to let a tropical edge
alone at the beginning of March.

Gateway, Hong Kong

for a whiter
porcelain-like
complexion,
cultivate
surfaces
that shatter
when dropped
keep
on high shelves
where nobody will
touch them
until some
special
guest comes
handles them
with care over
conversation
that is o so
polite
in public

the calisthenics of rain

1

every breeze is
a spirit moving
on the face
of water. This

heat undoes, says
let there un
be and it is
not, crushes

every thing to chaos
that might as well be
primordial. Breath
lifts a corner of it, says

let light be
now before
heat begins
again.

2

Locusts sing heat
today. The weight
of their song is meant

to remind me
air here is as
heavy with words

as ocean with
water. You could
drown in it, but

you can no more
take one word in
hand than you can

divide the sea
into drops
that compose it.

Words slip through
fingers like water,
and tipsy poets

have been lost
reaching for reflections
on the surface of them.

If you do not become
a fish, you must
tread water
until you learn
to swim, or
you will drown in it.

3

You must not imagine rain
liquid. It falls hard
shatters, showers
shrapnel. You will spend hours
digging splinters of it from
flesh exposed when it
burst on a crowd
that contained you,
unimagined.

4

That water is
a soft thing is
a lie. Listen
to it hammer
on the roof, hard
as steel in this
storm while sparrows
cower in the eaves
and every other
bird falls silent.

It has a sharp
edge, and it is
hard to be sure
it will not cut
through the fragile
tile of the roof
the way it cut

to bone when south
lit the fuse this morning.

It burns right through
umbrellas, fills
lungs, laughing
at the thought that
drowning is a slow
soft settling into sleep.

More like being
bludgeoned with an ax
and nothing you can
do to soften
the blows but hide
like sparrows who know
they have no power
to sing.

5

When they tell me old men
who use big brushes
to write in water
on public walkways
do it for exercise, I am astounded
at the calisthenics of rain.

Old men copy ancient poems
passersby know by heart
in delicate calligraphy
that will last until water

turns to air under the influence
of time and sun. Rain

writes new poems
in furious lines
that saturate the world
leave traces after floods
that remain on the tips of our tongues
though no one can say what they mean.

no denying it

Waiting is the only element
essential to a storm. Water
is not, though it adds drama

pooling through closed windows
at the ferry terminal when
a typhoon approaches.

Waves of it rolling when
the ship gets underway
could lead you to believe

it is the main attraction.
A little boy delighted to discover
a puddle for splashing

inside is sure of it, walks on it,
laughing. Fire
goes electric to keep

the shop vac roaring,
but a little flood creeps
across the floor in spite

of it while a sign tells us
what we know already of time
and the ferry to Shekou: waiting.

It is not like the gaudy display
of a Spring thunderstorm
on the plains that lights the sky

so you'd think day
nothing
but a series of gasps

between night's breaths
but there is no
denying it. Earth

is composed
of waiting.
The gravity of it

leads you to expect
turbulence no matter
where you fly

even when

Bird dances
on the roof
over my head. *This
is how to fly*, she says,

*even when you think
you have a place to stand.*

it goes without saying

Bai tou weng sways
on the long stalk
of an orange canna. There is
something to eat at the base
of the flower, and his
song stops while he turns his
attention to consuming
it. Locusts go on. Another
bulbul sings unseen
while *dizi* drifts over
from a loudspeaker
hidden somewhere. It goes
without saying the bird is
live. Some note in the songs
signals there is an old man
like the one swaying silent
singing – but not a trace
of a flute player
waiting in the wings.

all parallels and perpendiculars

A perfect arc of six leaves breaks
the pattern of paving stones, all
parallels and perpendiculars
monochrome under a rainbow
of falling weather. Six leaves in
seven colors, every one a chance
encounter of two pigments
and ten thousand variations
in a climate that never seems

to change. Acid rains etch
new patterns on old stone. Sun
bleaches what is not
in shade. Tree artists send roots
in all directions, add fault lines
to herringbone, lift stones
out of settled planes, work
in three dimensions

or more, like street people.
Past erupts through the plane
surface of the present. When
I stop for coffee, strangers
at the next table are discussing
complex systems. What are the odds
I will hear *Mandelbrot* in a random
conversation after admiring
the art of chance operations

on a long walk? Nothing alive is
perfectly parallel.

Only death abides perpendiculars.

year of the rat

1. Nanshan horoscope

Rat
scampers
across
the path
between
dogs who
take no
notice
and
walkers
so early
they have
no place
to go.

Someone left dinner
half finished in styrofoam
last night, and he found it before
the sweeper. So his belly is full
and he's in no hurry once
he gets to the other side.

Mornings like this
give him reason
to believe
it could be his year.

2. a dim sum of the day before

Four young rats sample a dim sum
of the day before in the trashcan
beside the path. They see no reason
to scatter when I pass. Another

I think older, maybe wiser
peers from the cover
of low vines a few steps further on.

When I pass again,
two cats hunting turn
at *miao,* but keep their distance.

Rain leaves something for everyone,
but next morning I see just one
rat fat as a pampered cat
dining *alfresco* between showers.

3. bourgeois joggers at five

I have never seen a corrupt official
gathering breakfast in the gaps between
impatiens on a morning walk. Rats count
on the scraps of our excess, but they work
for a living, consult watches for lost time when
I interrupt their routine. They
avoid contact. One never knows,
they know, what a stray might carry.

These fat rats are bourgeois joggers
at five, at their desks by seven.
They've learned to avoid
strangers, wash hands
again and again
to keep pandemics at bay.

4. a sacrament

Two rats playing
on the grass
by the walk

take note
of my passing,
a pause,

long enough

to determine I am nothing more
than a harmless *voyeur*
looking for a sign
in the ease
of their movement,
hoping to make sense

of the turning world.

A dog or a cat would demand
adjustment, not an old man
driven to distraction
who mistakes them
for a sacrament.

5. close

Cold hard
as fact
rat flat
under the wheel
knows perfectly well

death has always been
closer than the interval
between one breath
and another

when breath stops
and your heart
stops to think
about the next
beat, close as it is now.
Tail curves to shadow
the arc of the body
in one dimension
like a wry smile, says
just wait: you'll see.

water music

for the light

1

I come to China to learn
to walk away. Gray
kitten on a branch beyond my reach
cries, and I cannot coax him down.
He knows there is nothing

I can do, so I walk on, and he falls
silent. I'd like to think he found
some comfort in my voice
responding to his cry,
but he is still

treed, and I have done nothing.
The world is no less dangerous
for my words. He will tell his story,
put his feet on the ground
when he sees the time is right.

2

I come to China for the light, gray
soft through everyday
fog. The fog of every war settles
on this coast – power
speed sound

cities grow thick
with it, slow
to the chill consistency
of honey, set.

Everything moves
at the sticky sweet speed
of deliberate light, still
time.

Some days sun
glows dull through clouds
waiting to rain gray light
that will fill low paths
looking for a way
to ocean they remember
where these roads are.

Some days it shatters
into ten thousand
red shards on subtle
mist, scatters
across a whole
sky yellow to red, settles
finally to earth as dust
some god might spit on
to make a new man
to be fruitful and multiply
bodies of gray light

on dry land he names
so the god will know
how to address them.

3

I come to China for silence in a wall
of sound. There is no
denying the fire in
Lhasa, no
words for it.

4

I come to China for the leaves, always
Autumn. Kowloon in March, water
mirrors gray sky. They drop
green yellow orange red white
as the water of the fountain
swaying with waves
passing, milling
where there are edges. A brown one
falls in the center, bobs, does not appear
to move. But it is clinging to the edge of a
crowd an hour later, earth tone patch of sienna.

In Shenzhen, they scatter across
every walk over paving stone drones,
ragas for all hours, with the birds
who will sing for concrete eaves
when the trees are gone.

5

I come to China for the children
who say *hello* because they
like the sweet taste of two els
when they roll them on their tongues.

They never answer my poor
ni hao ma? But I taste *hao*
sweet in their laughter.

6

I come to China for the tricycle flower garden
that pedals past on a claustrophobic boulevard in
Nanshan after a Sunday walk, palm tree almost tall
enough to shade the rider on the leading edge of a dozen
potted plants in red and white, fragrance of lilies snaking
between buses through the crowd waiting for a break in
traffic to slip through before the light turns.

7

A man writes in water
on the walkway that echoes
Nan Shan's silhouette
walking south to the harbor
on Nan Hai Da Dao.
I step lightly
between characters,
glad I looked down.
This text will not last,

but I don't want to be
the one who crushes it

walking on water
without a thought
before it rises
silent on morning
heat into air.

8

A woman in black
with long black hair
takes hours to water
every plant on
the square
by hand.

She knows them
by name, and they
bring her flowers.

9

No one goes anywhere for any reason

but for love, drawn
by circles of friends, driven
by circles broken.

There is no place
but this.

a kind of meditation

The park is full of people raging
against silence. It is
a kind of meditation, this breaking
the smooth surface where day begins
by shouting across the lake to hear
your own voice answer, carrying
a radio with you so you will not get lost
in the sound of the world when
the chatter stops. Fish break the surface
of the lily pond when something they can eat
skates close on it. Ducks scoop what they need
off the surface, gliding. The crowd raging
in the park prepares for war. It is not
day that breaks, but the silence that precedes it.

one noble truth

for Long Xiaoying and Li Sen

Black cat sits
on the stone fence
of a temple worshiping
birds. I do not think
he is a Buddha
yet. Every time
a bird flies, he rises
with it, disappointed.

He has renounced every desire
but this – to take the body,
taste the blood
of god. But he
never leaps,
just sits, suffers
birds to fly.

bouganvillea

The one that fell
draws the eye more
than clusters pink
touched by blue
standing above
lines of green
on straight stems.

They take blue in,
nod to common
purple, but the one
that fell cannot bear
the weight of it.

The weight of it
embraces the whole
flower, cannot stop
at something so light
as the far end

of an imagined spectrum, insists
on the dark surface of a table
waiting for morning
coffee, on paving stones, on
gaps that open onto earth
waiting below

every line of sight.

no fear

East, moon crescent,
star, sea, time, sun.
Haze-softened red

you can look full
in the face
with no fear

of blindness.
Morning.

water music

1

Today the rhythm is rain's, stepping
on umbrellas that change the ways
people collide. The city
will not stop for it

but umbrellas demand
a different dance
on narrow steps

rain rearranges yellow
leaves on red stones
makes water music of dry brooms

shortens
my walk

Clouds break
sun rises
late, slips
into the softness
of it, stretches across
the whole cushion of the sky

2

After an hour of steady rain, each drop
is a perfect circle moving in an instant
on the surface of the water seeking
every other until it pauses and
a mirror rests on rust red paving stones.

3

Leaves fall
with rain. Pools
splash yellow
when children
jump in them.

Brown green red
yellow waves ripple
when each car passes.

And in the end
they soak right through
your skin. You feel

what trees feel
when they reach for rain
on days like this, when
every green thing is smiling.

twelve songs, two mornings

1

woman walking
on paving stone

ten thousand
cicadas crouching

mourning dove
distant

sparrows
chirping

bai tou bei
high in tree

foghorns

ferry sputters
to life

man on a cellphone
deals in Cantonese

heat so intense
you can hear

its low drone under
the whole scene

two birds hop on
translucent roof
over my head

tap a tune like dancing
on my grave

2

Four hours before sunrise,
two songs. A bird stretches
four notes across the tops of trees
between buildings, then rushes
four more into the time of one.
Eight notes count five.

Something sets off a car alarm.
Horn sounds senseless twelve times
loud, stops, long enough for a driver
to run in and out without turning
it off. Bird waits until I am certain
I know the pattern of his song

then stops at four. We laugh
at this surprise of silence.

In a Village Near Kunming

1

The whole population of the village
gathers at the door of a house
where a man squats with a makeshift scale
and a basket of wild mushrooms. He is
sorting them into a bucket a woman holds
in the vortex of the gathering crowd.

Fingers turn them this way and that for
a better look, while she sifts through
to find the right cap for each stem. You say
the more color the more poison.

The basket is a riot of earth
tones. I wonder what visions
those fingers have seen
caressing the flesh
measuring the poison
striking a balance

between what could kill you
and a soup to die for.

2

In a village near Kunming, two boys
fall in with our walk, listen
to our talk, but cannot place
the sound of it in a language
they know. One must be
a scholar of Greek. He repeats
what I say: *ba ba ba ba ba*, on his way
to naming me what almost every villager
in every village since Athens has named
every other stranger. To his friend, in words
I do not know, he must have said *they talk so fast,
but it sounds like nothing*, while I go on
ba ba ba ba ba, ba ba ba ba ba.

3

A dirt path just wide enough for an oxcart
breaks off a road not much wider. A boy
at the far end sees us walking and calls
hello. He starts for the road but runs back
when we turn. Young dog picks up our pace
and seems to think he might follow us
to whatever elsewhere we inhabit,
but he turns, contained, by the time
we reach the edge of the village.
He has no reason to believe beyond possible.

conversation

a hollow in the stone
forest, a conversation
of four frogs

each in his own pond
every call echoes
while it waits

for every other response

our own exile

Just this morning, I tried to explain
tortoiseshell, and the conversation
turned from cats to turtles to the ocean
while my mind wandered to D.H. Lawrence.

An orange tabby sunning on the street
warmed to your touch between his ears. Now
a tortoiseshell appears, a sign, but you
are not here, and pointing means nothing.

She is hungry enough to risk the presence
of a crowd for the taste of a steamed bun
while her sisters hide, dreaming of fish.

Another day, Tuku's *feeling low*
and the sound of Zimbabwe
has me thinking Mapfumo

while I sip Yunnan coffee
at Salvador's and we each dream
a failed revolution in our own exile.

a matter of sound

Frogs on Green Lake are a matter
of sound, what is not there
in the center of the center
of a ring of ripples in ripples near
a lily pad. Two white ducks weave
in and out among lotus leaves greener
than the lake. Here and there
a blossom rises, pink, white,
willow branches lean into water.

Walkers clap
to tap,
tap, tap
of foot
on stone,
slp, slp, slp
of sandals sliding.

Someone chants loud
and his own voice answers
from the other side. *Dizi*
drifts over with mosquitoes.

Morning

for Xinwen

the city still
sleeping. It rises
as I walk
on air lighter
than the sea.

Dogs that walk the same way
every morning speak in their way.
Children follow them on their way
to school. There is the same dance
here of sweepers and *qigong*
in the park. Sitting
by the lake, I lift my feet
for a broom, listen.

Music rises with the city.

signs

小心你的头
be careful with your head
      sign on an escalator in Nanshan

mind the gap
a little heart
with your head
no exit

that is all

Steven Schroeder received his Ph.D. in Ethics and Society from the University of Chicago in 1982. He is the co-founder, with composer Clarice Assad, of the Virtual Artists Collective (a "virtual" gathering of musicians, poets, and visual artists – vacpoetry.org), which has published five full-length poetry collections each year since it began in 2004. He teaches at the University of Chicago in Asian Classics and the Basic Program of Liberal Education for Adults and at Shenzhen University in China.

His work has appeared or is forthcoming in *After Hours, AmarilloBay, Cha: An Asian Literary Journal; Concho River Review,* the *Cresset, Druskininkai Poetic Fall 2005, Georgetown Review, Karamu, Macao Closer, Mid-America Poetry Review, Poetry East, Poetry Macao, Rambunctious Review, Rhino, Shichao, Sichuan Literature, Texas Review, TriQuarterly* and other literary journals. He has published two chapbooks, *Theory of Cats* and *Revolutionary Patience,* and three full-length collections, *Fallen Prose, The Imperfection of the Eye,* and *Six Stops South.*

www.ingramcontent.com/pod-product-compliance
Lightning Source LLC
Chambersburg PA
CBHW031202090426
42736CB00009B/760